Welcome To The Deepest Book

The 200 deep questions Book is an easy way to record all your secrets and an interactive journal that invites you to face life's big questions. Because it's plenty of deep and private questions that only the owner has the right to see. So when you finish filling the book don't think about keeping it, you should tear it, burn it, or smash it, after writing. Some questions are fun, some are deep and some are just plain random.

DETAILS :

PART N° 1 "THE FIRST"

Always the first love or the first success and failure has a special taste, So we created a list of "THE FIRST" for you to bring back your memories.

PART N° 2 "WH Questions"

This part contains general questions about yourself, just be honest with each question to find out more about yourself.

THIS BOOK BELONGS TO

This book contains deep and private questions that only the owner has the right to see.
So, when you finish filling the book, don't think about keeping it, you should tear it, burn it, or smash it

PART N° 1
"THE FIRST"

Always the first experience, the first love, or the first success and failure has a special taste. So we created a list of "the first" for you to bring back your memories

"My First"

My First BF/GF:

My First Love:

My First Kiss:

My first success that I remember:

My first Friend:

My First Crush:

My First Night out Home:

My First Job:

My First thing I do every night:

My First secret:

My First toy:

My First pet:

My first failure in school:

My First cooking:

My First smoke:

My First school:

My First film:

My First trip:

My First car:

My First Smartphone:

My First thing I do every day:

My First night alone:

My First game:

My First social media:

My First dream:

My First bike:

My First book I remember reading:

My First watch:

My First teacher:

My First computer:

My First draw:

My First swim:

My First online shopping:

My First fear:

My First anniversary:

PART N° 2
"WH QUESTIONS"

General questions about yourself
Just be honest with each question to find out more about yourself

Do you want to be different in the world?

Do you think experiences are important?

What is the best city in the world for you? Why?

What is the worst place in the world for you? Why?

What is your favorite Deep movie?

What is your favorite book?

What is your favorite series?

What are the best events that happened to you in the last year?

What makes you different from others?

How can you describe your personality?

Describe your relationship with your parents?

What makes you nervous?

What's the worst for you?

What trait do others envy you?

What skill do you wish you had?

How do you wish to be remembered?

How would your best friend describe you in five words?

How would you summarize your life purpose?

Are you an introvert or an extrovert?

Where do you see yourself in two years?

Do you think money is very important in your life?

What makes you sad?

What are you afraid of?

What is your personal strategy for being happy?

Who are your five idols?

How do you spend your money?

What is the best advice you have received? Why?

What's the worst advice you've received? Why?

3 movies that make you cry every time?

What does your perfect day look like?

What do you do to de-stress?

What are the qualities that you like in others?

Are you making decisions quickly?

What is the best achievement in your life?

Do you think technology is important for you?

What is your favorite quote? Write it here

What do you do to keep your friends close?

How do you react with your mistakes?

What do you do in your free time?

Who inspires you? Why?

Who influenced you?

What is your hidden talent?

Are you proud of your life?

What are the 3 biggest lessons you have ever learned in life?

If you could be famous for an hour, what would you do?

Which of your parents do you like the most?

What is the best and worst period of your life?

What makes you feel frustrated? Why?

Who are 3 people you can talk to about anything?

Have you ever lost someone close to you?

What would you do if your parents did not like your partner?

Do you like to plan things out or are you impulsive?

Do you love cats?

Do you think you will be rich?

What are your favorite top 10 stars?

How would you describe your dad?

What are the 3 craziest things you've ever done?

What are five things you value most about a person?

What would you do if you were alone?

Who was your favorite teacher? Why?

What is your shortest friendship?

What is your longest friendship?

Do you like dogs?

What are the five things you wish you knew how to do?

What can't money buy for you?

What are your 5 favorite actresses?

What is your greatest challenge?

Are you happy alone or in a relationship?

Do you want to be famous?

What is your preferred age? Why?

If you are in a bad mood do you prefer to be alone?

What would you not give up for $ 5000000 in cash?

Do you usually do whatever you want or not?

How would you describe yourself?

What did your past teach you?

Do you prefer giving or receiving gifts?

If a genie granted you 3 wishes, what would you wish for?

How would you describe your grandparent?

How would you describe your luck?

Where are you going next summer?

What is the weather you prefer?

What's your favorite food?

What would you do if you had 10 million dollars?

What languages do you speak?

Who is your best friend and why?

Where do you wish to live now?

What is your best and worst childhood memory?

What is your best year of school? Why?

Do you believe in true love, or love at first sight? Why?

What is the best way to motivate you?

What is your long-term goal?

What are you ashamed of?

Do you consider your dad and mom as friends?

Do you prefer to save money or invest?

What is the most important thing for you in a relationship and why?

When was your best birthday? Why?

What do you prefer: family events or alone time?

When was your perfect vacation?

Do you have any phobias?

What are your 3 greatest qualities?

How do your friends describe you?

Do you believe in a soul mate?

What do you do when you hurt someone?

If your life was a movie or a book what would be the title to it?

When did you cause the most harm to yourself?

What's the biggest change you've ever made that made you the most proud of yourself?

Think about the people you love the most in your life, what do you do for them?

Where do you go when you want to be alone?

What Is the Biggest Lie you have ever told?

Do you steal money from your parents?

Have you ever cheated on your friend?

What is your biggest regret?

What is the hardest decision you've ever made?

What is the biggest risk you've ever taken?

What was the most difficult time in your life?

If you had to eat only one thing for a month, what would it be?

What was your dream job when you were young?

Tell me about one of your dreams

Tell me about the worst date you've ever had.

If you could change one thing about yourself, what would it be?

Have you ever snooped on your friend?

Are you arrogant?

What do you do when you don't have the courage to do something?

What makes you laugh every time?

Who Has Completely Lost Your Respect?

Have you ever had an operation?

Do You Have Any Enemies?

What is the best gift you have received?

Are you afraid of getting old?

Do you want to get married someday?

What is the darkest thing you've never told anybody?

Is there anything that you find extremely disturbing in the house?

What insect scares you?

Is there an activity that calms you down?

What is your favorite song and why?

What Kind Of People Do You Dislike?

What is scene in a movie has evoked the most feelings out of you? WHY

What makes you feel like you need to be alone?

What can you never forgive?

What can someone do to make you feel appreciated?

What advice would you like to give to others?

Who is the most important person in your life?

What's the best thing that has happened to you this year?

Why did you cry the last time?

Have you ever cried with tears of joy?

If I asked you at age 10 what you wanted to be when you grew up, what would you say?

The last time …

The last time I cried

The last time i said i love you

The last time i danced

The last time i laughed

The last time I lost a loved one

The last time I went to the cinema

The last time I felt sad

The last

The last time I felt love

The last time i lied

The last song I listened to

My last trip

My last shopping

the last time I felt a success

The last time i said thank you

"This or that"

Is an easy to play word game where you have to choose between two things. Even if you don't like any of the options, you have to choose one.

Example:

Google | Bing

Going out at night	stay at home
Vanilla	strawberry
Horror movie	comedy
Car	bicycle
Tablet	mobile
Soccer	basketball
Milk	coffee
Pizza	hamburger
Fries	chocolate

Tart	cake
Apple	banana
Crepe	waffle
Breakfast	dinner
Night	morning
Passenger	diver
Fast food	health food
Train	airplane
City	countryside

Tattoos	piercings
Book	movie
Family	friends
Beach	pool
Christmas	birthday
Flying	turning invisible
Ice cream	hotdogs
Big class	small class
Recent history	ancient history

Phone call	text
ios	android
Email	letter
Coffee cup	thermos
Meat	vegetable
Ocean	Mountains
Winter	summer
Speak	listen
Love	money

Thank you for choosing "200 Deep Questions Book". Please leave us a Good review. It will only take a minute, but it will make a huge difference to us. Thank you!"

Made in the USA
Coppell, TX
05 August 2024

35597888R00056